GETTING TO KNOW THE WORLD'S GREATEST
INVENTORS & SCIENTISTS

JANE
GOODALL
Researcher Who Champions Chimps

WRITTEN AND ILLUSTRATED BY MIKE VENEZIA

CHILDREN'S PRESS®
AN IMPRINT OF SCHOLASTIC INC.
NEW YORK TORONTO LONDON AUCKLAND SYDNEY
MEXICO CITY NEW DELHI HONG KONG
DANBURY, CONNECTICUT

Reading Consultant: Nanci R. Vargus, Ed.D., Assistant Professor, School of Education, University of Indianapolis

Photographs © 2010: Corbis Images/Bettmann: 10; Everett Collection, Inc.: 12 (Advertising Archive), 25, 29 (CSU Archives), 13 (Mary Evans Picture Library); Jane Goodall Institute: 18, 20, 23; National Geographic Image Collection: 27 top (Jane Goodall), 6, 7 (Frans Lanting), 8, 27 bottom, 31 (Michael Nichols), 3, 22, 26 (Hugo Van Lawick), 30 (Steve Winter); Photolibrary/Corbis: 16.

Colorist for illustrations: Andrew Day

Library of Congress Cataloging-in-Publication Data

Venezia, Mike.
  Jane Goodall : researcher who champions chimps / written and illustrated by Mike Venezia.
      p. cm.
  Includes index.
  ISBN-13: 978-0-531-23731-1 (lib. bdg.)   978-0-531-22352-9 (pbk.)
  ISBN-10: 0-531-23731-1 (lib. bdg.)   0-531-22352-3 (pbk)
  1. Goodall, Jane, 1934—Juvenile literature. 2. Primatologists—England—Biography—Juvenile literature. 3. Women primatologists—England—Biography—Juvenile literature. 4. Chimpanzees—Tanzania—Gombe Stream National Park—Juvenile literature. I. Title.
  QL31.G58V465 2010
  590.92—dc22
  [B]
                              2009030213

1 2 3 4 5 6 7 8 9 10 R 19 18 17 16 15 14 13 12 11 10

Researcher Jane Goodall spent many years observing chimpanzees in Africa. Over time, she gained the trust of many of these wild animals.

Valerie Jane Morris-Goodall was born on April 3, 1934, in London, England. When she grew up, she shortened her name to Jane Goodall. Jane Goodall has spent more than fifty years learning about wild animals, particularly chimpanzees. Her work has helped protect chimps from becoming **endangered** and has preserved their jungle homes.

For as long as she could remember,
Jane Goodall had a wonderful dream.
It was to travel to Africa and somehow
find a way to work with animals in
their natural surroundings.

Jane never gave up on her dream. She
eventually became an **ethologist**—a scientist
who studies animal behavior. Jane made
remarkable discoveries that showed that
chimpanzees are much more like human
beings than anyone ever imagined.

In 1960, when Jane Goodall began studying wild chimps, hardly anyone knew a thing about how they lived naturally in the jungle. Most researchers had studied only laboratory chimpanzees or those kept as pets. After years of observing chimps in African forests, Jane revealed things about them that totally surprised scientists.

Jane Goodall discovered that chimpanzees, like humans, can make and use tools. Here a chimpanzee uses a plant stem as a "fishing pole" for termites.

Goodall also discovered that chimpanzees engage in warfare. She observed a "war" between two groups of male chimps that lasted for four years. Here an angry chimpanzee threatens to throw a rock.

One amazing discovery was that chimpanzees were able to make and use simple tools. Scientists had thought only humans could do this. Later, Jane learned that chimps, like humans, sometimes go to war and fight deadly battles to protect or take over territory! Also, scientists had always thought that chimpanzees ate only plants, fruits, and small insects. Jane discovered that chimpanzees sometimes hunted animals and ate meat.

Jane had very interesting parents. Her dad was a skilled racecar driver. Because he was often away at one race or another, Jane spent most of her time with her mom. Mrs. Goodall taught Jane all about nature. They often spent hours in their garden, where Mrs. Goodall would point out interesting facts about birds, insects, and small animals.

Jane Goodall has always loved animals. She still has Jubilee, the chimpanzee doll that was her constant companion when she was a child.

Mrs. Goodall was not the least bit squeamish when it came to her daughter's interest in nature. Once Jane brought worms and dirt in from the garden and made a worm house under her pillow! Jane's nanny freaked out when she saw the wiggly mess, but Mrs. Goodall calmly explained to Jane that the worms would be better off back in their natural surroundings.

During World War II, many children were evacuated from London for their safety (above). Jane and her mother left London to live with Jane's grandmother in Bournemouth in the south of England.

In 1939, when Jane was five years old, Germany's Nazi army began invading European countries, and World War II began. London was in constant danger of being bombed by the Germans. Mr. Goodall joined the British army right away. Jane, her little sister Judy, and Mrs. Goodall left London and went to live with Jane's grandmother in Bournemouth, England, where it was much safer.

Bournemouth was the perfect place for Jane. It was near the sea. There were rocky cliffs, pine forests, and plenty of little forest animals she could observe. There was also a big and wild garden where Jane and her friends would meet. One summer, they formed a nature club. Their goal was to study nature and raise money to help take care of old horses. Sometimes, for fun, the girls would paint numbers on garden snails and enter them in races.

As a child, Jane loved to read animal stories, including Rudyard Kipling's animal tales (right) and the Tarzan books (opposite page).

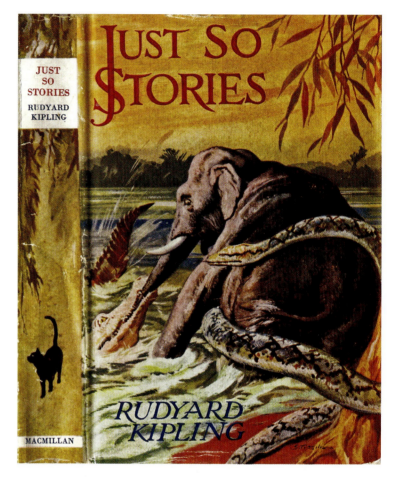

Jane's lifelong love of reading began while she was growing up in Bournemouth. She was fascinated by stories in which people and animals were able to talk to each other. Jane read all of the Dr. Doolittle books, Rudyard Kipling's animal stories, and the exciting adventures of Tarzan of the Apes.

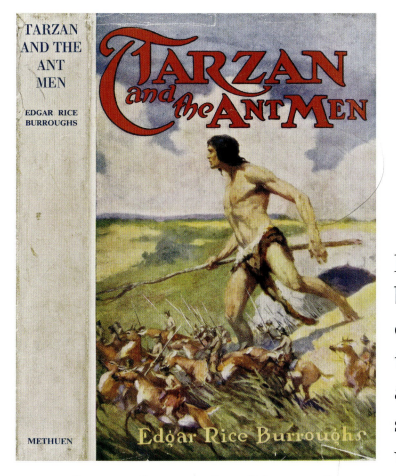

Like the heroes in these books, Jane was determined to travel to the jungle and get as close as she could to the wild animals there. Jane always had lots of pets. One dog, named Rusty, was her favorite. Jane taught him all kinds of tricks. Rusty seemed to be able to think things out. His behavior made Jane wonder how much animals really knew.

Jane Goodall always did well in school. By the time she graduated from high school, World War II had ended. Jane decided to go to a secretarial school in London, where she learned typing, **shorthand,** and bookkeeping. These skills helped her get a series of interesting jobs, including working for a filmmaking company. But Jane never forgot about her dream. She spent a lot of her spare time reading up on animals, observing them at the zoo, and visiting London's museum of natural history.

Then, a lucky break came along that changed everything. Clo Mange, an old friend of Jane's, had moved from England to a farm her parents had bought in Kenya, in eastern Africa. Clo invited Jane to visit the farm. This was a perfect opportunity for Jane. She worked extra hard to raise money for the trip. Finally, on March 13, 1957, she boarded a passenger ship and headed off to the land of her dreams.

JANE GOODALL'S TRIP FROM ENGLAND TO AFRICA

ENGLAND

RUSSIA

EUROPE

THE MIDDLE EAST

AFRICA

KENYA

During her first visit to Africa, Jane was thrilled by the native animals, like giraffes, that she saw there.

Africa was everything Jane had ever hoped for. After she arrived at Clo's farm, Jane saw hyenas, gazelles, and giraffes running free. Right away, she got a job as a typist in the nearby city of Nairobi (nye-ROW-bee). The office job gave Jane a chance to make money until she could figure out a way to work with animals.

Jane was always talking about her favorite subject. Everyone she met knew of her interest in animals. Finally, someone suggested that Jane contact Louis Leakey, the famous **anthropologist** and **paleontologist.** Dr. Leakey and his wife, Mary, were known for discovering **fossils** that provided clues about when animals and human beings first began to appear on Earth. Louis Leakey was also the **curator** of a natural history museum in Nairobi. Right away, Jane made an appointment to see him.

Louis liked Jane. He was impressed with her knowledge of African animals and their habits. Louis decided to hire Jane to work as an assistant at the museum. But before Jane started her job, Louis and Mary took her along on an exciting adventure.

Jane (right) with the Leakeys at Olduvai Gorge in 1957

They traveled together to the Olduvai (OHL-duh-vye) Gorge in Tanzania (tan-zuh-NEE-uh). This was the Leakeys' favorite spot to search for fossils and tools of our human **ancestors.** In the evenings, sitting around the campfire, Jane heard hyenas crying out and lions roaring. Jane loved it!

To learn more about the similarities between humans and chimps, Dr. Leakey, pictured here with Jane, wanted Jane to observe wild champanzees in Tanzania.

After the group returned to Nairobi, Jane thought for a while about becoming a paleontologist. But eventually she decided to stick with her dream. Jane still wanted to get as close as she could to live animals. She wanted to live like her childhood heroes, Tarzan and Dr. Doolittle.

One day, Jane heard Louis talking about a group of chimpanzees living in a remote area of Africa. He wanted someone to observe them. Chimpanzees and humans are closely related to each other. Louis thought studying chimpanzees might provide clues about how early humans developed. Louis decided that Jane Goodall might be the perfect person to send into the deepest part of Africa to learn all she could about chimps.

At Gombe, Jane sometimes climbed into trees so that she could see over tall grasses and have a better view of the chimpanzees.

Jane couldn't believe Louis would consider her for such an important job. First of all, she had no college degree or special training. Plus, it was dangerous for a young woman to go off into the forests of Africa.

Louis Leakey knew there was something special about Jane Goodall. He had full confidence in her. In 1960, after preparing for the trip, Jane traveled to the north end of Lake Tanganyika (tan-guhn-YEE-kuh) to an area called the Gombe (GAHM-be) Stream Game Reserve (now called Gombe Stream National Park). It was the land of chimpanzees!

Jane wasn't totally alone at Gombe. Her mom came for a short time to help her set up camp. She also had a guide and a cook. As soon as she could, Jane went out to begin exploring.

Jane and her mother at the Gombe Stream camp in 1960

At first, chimpanzees wouldn't come anywhere near Jane. They were afraid of her. The chimps had never seen humans before. For months, Jane had to study them from a distance. It was hard work. Jane often had to crawl and wiggle her way through thick underbrush to get near the chimps. She never knew when she might run into a venomous snake or a sleeping lion. Sometimes she slept outdoors near a group of chimps so she could observe them when they woke up early in the morning.

Finally, one day, a chimp Jane had named David Greybeard came into camp and helped himself to some bananas. This was a great day for Jane. It was the first sign that the chimps were feeling more relaxed around her.

As the chimpanzees got used to Jane's presence, they allowed her to get closer and closer. David Greybeard (above) was the first chimp to trust Jane enough to come right up to her.

Naming the chimps she studied was one of the first remarkable things Jane did. Up until this time, ethologists identified animals by giving them numbers. They studied animals only as scientific subjects. But Jane saw chimps also as individuals, each with his or her own special look and personality. Soon, Jane was able to get close not only to David Greybeard, but also to other chimps that she had named, including Goliath, William, Old Flo, all Flo's children, and lots of others.

An infant chimpanzee reaches out to touch Jane's hand.

Once, Jane saw David Greybeard stripping leaves off a twig. He dipped the bare twig into a termite mound to fish for and collect the tasty insects. He had actually made and used a tool to gather food! Over time, Jane saw chimps doing other humanlike things, such as hugging, kissing, and even tickling each other.

Jane spent many years watching Old Flo, an excellent mother.

Jane watches Fifi pick bugs out of a baby chimp's fur.

Jane Goodall started to gain attention for her discoveries. Scientists, including Louis Leakey, were surprised and excited to find out how much humans and chimpanzees had in common.

In 1961, Jane was offered the opportunity to study ethology at Cambridge University in England. Over the next few years, she went back and forth between England and Africa while she worked on her **doctoral degree.**

During this time, a nature photographer named Hugo van Lawick came to Gombe to

Jane with Hugo van Lawick and their son, Grub, in Tanzania in the mid-1970s

photograph Jane's work with the chimps. Jane and Hugo eventually fell in love, and they got married in 1964. In 1967, they had a son, also named Hugo, whom they affectionately nicknamed Grub. Grub lived an exciting life growing up with his parents in the African jungle. Jane wrote a book about his adventures called *Grub, the Bush Baby*.

Because chimpanzees are so similar to humans, scientists have sometimes used them as **lab animals** (above). Jane accepts that it is sometimes necessary to experiment on animals for medical research. But she has encouraged scientists to find alternatives to live-animal research, and insists that scientists treat lab chimps humanely.

Jane spent many years doing research on chimps and writing books about her discoveries. Today she spends much of her time working with the Jane Goodall Institute, an organization she founded. Its goal is to show how each and every one of us can help improve the environment for all living things on Earth. Jane has worked hard to set up shelters for orphaned chimpanzees and protect other chimps from being kept in medical research labs.

Over the years, much of the jungle forest near the Gombe Stream National Park has been lost to the logging business and to a growing human population. Jane has led an effort to protect chimp habitats there by **reforesting** parts of the area.

Jane puts a lot of hope for the future in children. She believes young people who learn to understand the environment and respect animals will have the power to change the world for the better when they grow up.

Jane Goodall meets with young members of Roots and Shoots, her worldwide program to help kids learn what they can do to help protect the environment.

Glossary

ancestor (AN-sess-tur) An early type of animal from which later kinds have evolved

anthropologist (an-thruh-POL-uh-jist) A person who studies the ways of life of people around the world

curator (KYOO-ray-tur) The person in charge of a museum or art gallery

doctoral degree (DOK-tur-uhl di-GREE) The highest degree given by universities

endangered (en-DAYN-jurd) In danger of becoming extinct

ethologist (ee-THAL-uh-jist) A person who studies animal behavior

fossil (FOSS-uhl) The remains or traces of an animal or plant from millions of years ago, preserved as rock

lab animal (LAB AN-uh-muhl) An animal that is experimented on for scientific or medical research

paleontologist (pale-ee-uhn-TOL-uh-jist) A person who studies the science of ancient life forms, as known from fossils

reforest (ree-FOR-est) To replant trees in a place where all the original trees were cut down or destroyed

shorthand (SHORT-hand) A system of writing symbols instead of words; it is used for taking notes quickly

Index